Money in Sports

Nick Hunter

Heinemann Library
Chicago, Illinois

www.capstonepub.com
Visit our website to find out more information about Heinemann-Raintree books.

To order:
☎ Phone 888-454-2279
▭ Visit www.capstonepub.com to browse our catalog and order online.

Edited by Adrian Vigliano and Claire Throp
Designed by Richard Parker
Picture research by Ruth Blair
Originated by Capstone Global Library Ltd
Printed and bound in China by Leo Paper
  Products Ltd

15 14 13 12 11
10 9 8 7 6 5 4 3 2 1

Library of Congress Cataloging-in-Publication Data
Hunter, Nick.
  Money in sports / Nick Hunter.
    p. cm.—(Ethics of sports)
  Includes bibliographical references and index.
  ISBN 978-1-4329-5977-7 (hb)—ISBN 978-1-4329-5982-1 (pb) 1. Professional sports—Economic aspects. 2. Sports—Economic aspects. 3. Sports—Moral and ethical aspects. I. Title.
  GV716.H86 2012
  338.47796—dc22   2011014607

Acknowledgments
We would like to thank the following for permission to reproduce photographs: Corbis pp. 7 (© Alinari Archives), 10 (© Gregg Newton), 12 (© PCN), 15 (© AAP Image/Martin Philbey), 17 (© Luis Blanco/ZUMA Press), 18 (© Zeng Yi/Xinhua Press), 21 (© Diego Azubel/epa), 23 (© Mike Hutchings/Reuters), 28 (© Icon Sports Media), 31 (© Bettmann), 35 top (© Tom Berg/Icon SMI), 35 bottom (© Mike McGinnis/ZUMA Press), 37 (© Eva-Lotta Jansson), 39 (© John Sommers II/Reuters), 40 (© Jerome Prevost/TempSport), 43 (© Diego Azubel/epa), 45 (© Finbarr O'Reilly/Reuters), 47 (© Chen Kai/Xinhua Press), 49 (© Bettmann), 50 (© Paul Childs Action Images Pool/epa), 51 (© Robin Alam/Icon SMI), 53 (© Greig Cowie/BPI); Getty Images pp. 9 (Bob Thomas/Popperfoto), 25 (Matthew Peters/Manchester United), 32 (Koichi Kamoshida); Shutterstock pp. 4 (© Rick Becker-Leckrone), 5 (© fstockfoto), 20 (© digitalsport-photoagency), 27 (© photofriday).

Cover photograph of a Formula One race reproduced with permission of Corbis (© Schlegelmilch).

We would like to thank Shawn E. Klein for his invaluable help in the preparation of this book.

Every effort has been made to contact copyright holders of any material reproduced in this book. Any omissions will be rectified in subsequent printings if notice is given to the publisher.

Disclaimer
All the Internet addresses (URLs) given in this book were valid at the time of going to press. However, due to the dynamic nature of the Internet, some addresses may have changed, or sites may have changed or ceased to exist since publication. While the author and publisher regret any inconvenience this may cause readers, no responsibility for any such changes can be accepted by either the author or the publisher.

CONTENTS

Some words are printed in bold, **like this**. You can find out what they mean by looking in the glossary.

THE ESSENCE OF SPORTS

What do you think of when you hear the word "sports"? Do you think of playing basketball or soccer at school or in a park with friends? Or do you think of top sports stars living a luxurious lifestyle that most of us can only dream of?

Sports are both of these things, and more. Young people playing basketball may be dreaming of being like the heroes they see on television or in a packed stadium. The stars were once just like the people in the park, learning the skills that would one day bring them fame and fortune. For most people, playing sports has little to do with money. People play sports because they love them, because they are a good form of exercise, and because of the friendships that can be made while playing sports.

These teenagers may be dreaming of being like the stars they see on television. But money is not the reason why they play sports.

Elite sports

Money is one part of many **elite** sports. But most athletes train not for riches, but rather for the achievement and honor of being the best in their sports. For many of these sports, the ultimate goal is to become world champion or win a gold medal at the Olympic Games.

However, many people also earn their living from sports. In addition to athletes, this includes people who manage the business side of sports or work in one of the many other jobs connected with sports. A tiny percentage of people earn enough money from sports to be very wealthy.

The question of money

This book will explore many of the ways in which money and sports are linked together. It will look at how money makes many sports possible, particularly the **professional** sports shown on television. It will also examine whether sports have become too much about money and whether, in some cases, money has started to become more important than the sports themselves.

Where does the money come from?

When you read about the wealthy lifestyles of your favorite sports stars, does it seem like this has nothing to do with your own life? In fact, there would be no money in sports without ordinary fans like you.

- Fans buy tickets to watch the stars, and they also spend money on **merchandise** such as T-shirts and jerseys.

- Television companies pay a lot of money to be able to show sports on television. Without fans, there would be no one to watch.

- **Advertisers** and **sponsors** pay money to sports stars and teams because they know that they can sell their product or get their message across to many people through sports.

So, without you, and millions of people like you, athletes would not be paid at all, let alone receive the riches that top stars in many sports can earn.

Without fans to buy tickets, there would be very little money in sports.

The path to professional sports

The story of money and sports goes back thousands of years, and the two have been linked as long as people have played sports.

Today, sports are something that many of us do or watch in our free time. Many people in the past had very little leisure time, so sports were only a small part of their lives. The people who did have time for sports were often wealthier people who could afford not to work all the time. There were also two other reasons why sports developed in the ancient world: religion and training for war.

Ancient Greece

Religion was the main reason for the founding of the Olympic Games in ancient Greece, which were held in the sacred grove of Zeus at Olympia (see box at right). Other sporting events in ancient Greece also honored gods and goddesses, such as the Panathenaic Games held by the people of Athens, which honored the goddess Athena.[1]

Although the reason for ancient Greek sports was to honor the gods, money played a part, too. This was especially true in chariot racing. Chariots were pulled by a team of horses, which were expensive to train and feed. So wealthy people usually owned the chariots. Chariot racing was a dangerous business, and the rich owners employed other people to do the dangerous job of racing the chariots.[3]

MONEY AND THE ANCIENT OLYMPICS

The Olympic Games were first staged at Olympia, in Greece, in 776 BCE. Although ancient Greek athletes could earn money, the only prize at the Olympics was a crown of olive branches. Fans might also arrange for a statue to be made to honor the champion. However, when Olympic champions returned to their home state, they would be showered with gifts and riches.[2]

Gladiators

Religion was also involved in the origin of the ancient Romans' best-known contribution to the history of sports: the gladiator. The first gladiators appeared as part of funerals, to honor dead warriors. In later years, contests were staged in which gladiators fought against each other and against wild beasts. These contests were held in huge amphitheaters, or arenas for public entertainment.

The idea that people could be deliberately killed in the name of sports seems brutal. But to the Romans, a visit to the Colosseum was much the same as watching a football game would be to us today.

Wealthy and powerful Romans paid for these games, in an attempt to gain power and influence with the people. Gladiators were often criminals or slaves. Fighting could make them rich and famous, but it was a short career, and death was rarely far away.[4] A few lucky gladiators were so successful that they were granted their freedom.[5]

Sports and warfare

In ancient times, and for many centuries afterward, sports were also about preparing for war. Many of today's sports, from javelin throwing to fencing and archery, have their origins in military training. Other sports tended to be organized locally, and they were usually only part of religious feasts held when most people were not working. Only the wealthiest people could afford to enjoy sports at other times.

Modern sports

Many of the sports that are popular today were established in the 1700s and 1800s. Many of these developed in the wealthier classes, particularly in Britain's private schools such as Eton and Rugby, the only school to have given its name to a major sport. Versions of soccer had been played since ancient times, but these were combined in Britain in the 1840s to become modern soccer.[6] Although soccer came from the same private schools as other sports, it soon became known as the people's game. These sports were strictly **amateur**, because those who played them had no need to earn money.

Other sports, such as football and basketball, developed in U.S. colleges.[7] Basketball was invented by physical education instructor James Naismith of New England as a sport for his students to play inside during cold winters. Baseball developed from the game of rounders with several teams playing in the New York area around 1845.

Professional players

Starting in the late 1700s, the **Industrial Revolution** changed societies in Britain and later spread to North America and the rest of Europe. More people moved to cities to work in factories. Sports became an increasingly popular form of entertainment in these cities, and teams were formed for sports like baseball and soccer.

At first, these teams were made up of amateurs who played when they were not at work, usually on Saturday afternoons. Money began to come into the games as people paid to watch local teams play. Teams started using some of this money to attract skilled players who could not otherwise afford to train and play for free.

In the late 1800s, it was finally agreed that players in British soccer could be paid. The first professional baseball league started in 1871. In these early days, power was with the team owners. Playing professional sports could bring fame and glory, but it was unlikely to bring much money to athletes.

As professionals appeared in more sports, tension developed between paid players and amateurs who were unpaid. For purists, the idea that people would only play because they were being paid was not in the true spirit of sports. At the same time, for many professional athletes, being paid was the only way they could afford to continue. Separate organizations developed in some sports for amateurs and professionals. Professional sports such as baseball and soccer attracted working people to their games in big industrial cities.

One of the most popular sports in the world—soccer (called "football" outside of the United States)—began in Britain. The Harrow soccer team, dressed in full team uniforms, are seen here in 1868.

The global spread of sports

After professional and amateur sports were established in the 1800s, they started to spread around the world. U.S. sports spread to areas that were under U.S. political influence. For example, baseball became a popular sport in Cuba and Japan. Soccer established itself more widely around the world than any other sport, partly because of its simple rules and because the only equipment needed was a ball. **Cricket** spread to countries that were part of the **British Empire**, including Australia, India, and South Africa.

In the later years of the 1900s, interest in sports spread farther around the globe because of **media** coverage, and also because of attempts by sports businesses to expand their fan base into new countries or "markets" (see pages 32–33).

The spread of basketball

Basketball became established around the world in more recent history. The Barcelona Olympics in 1992 were the first Olympic Games at which professional basketball players were allowed to play. The U.S. national team, which was made up of National Basketball Association (NBA) stars, was called the "Dream Team." It won easily against the mostly amateur players from the rest of the world. The fact that the world's best players were now playing at the Olympics helped basketball grow as an international sport.

The U.S. basketball "Dream Team" won gold at the Barcelona Olympics in 1992.

Making money

During the 1900s, most top sports professionals embraced the idea of sports as a moneymaking profession. Huge stadiums could hold up to 100,000 people to watch the biggest events. Millions of people began to follow sports, first in newspapers and on the radio, and later on live television coverage from around the world. As the money poured in, the idea that athletes should compete strictly out of "love" (the literal meaning of the French word *amateur*) went out of fashion.

The Olympic Games continued to value the idea of amateur athletes well after many other sports organizations had accepted the idea of professional athletes. However, it became increasingly clear that many Olympic athletes were amateurs in name only. In some countries, such as the **Soviet Union**, athletes were officially members of the military, but they were effectively paid as full-time athletes. In other countries, athletes received money for making public "appearances," or they received training **scholarships** to support them while they trained full-time.

> "The Olympic movement today is a revolt against 20th century **materialism**—a devotion to the cause and not the reward."[8]
>
> Avery Brundage, president of the International Olympic Committee (IOC) from 1952 to 1972, who believed that allowing only amateur athletes was an essential part of the Olympics. However, fewer than 20 years after the end of Brundage's period as IOC president, professionals were allowed to compete in the Olympics.

In the 1980s, the Olympics changed its view. It was decided that the world's best athletes should compete at the Games—and that meant professionals, too. Today, most Olympic sports allow professional athletes, although there are still some restrictions.[9]

Recent developments

Rugby union players were amateurs until 1995. Since their sport became professional, the players have been able to concentrate full-time on rugby.

In the early days of professional sports, power was very much with the people who owned the teams. That has changed in recent years, as players have recognized that the spectacle of sports would not exist without them (see box at right).

BASEBALL STRIKES

One sport that has seen a dramatic shift in the balance of power between owners and players is baseball. From the 1970s onward, the Major League Baseball Players Association (MLBPA) organized several **strikes**. The longest was in 1994–95, when 921 games were canceled because of a strike. The strike also stopped the World Series for the first time since 1904. This strike was begun in reaction to plans to put a limit on what teams could spend on **salaries**.

These strikes and the power of the MLBPA is one reason why the average salary in Major League Baseball rose from $41,000 in 1974 ($180,000 in today's money) to $3.3 million in 2010.[10]

WHO'S WHO IN MONEY AND SPORTS

There are two kinds of people who are essential in professional sports: the player and the spectator. However, there are many other people who make money from sports either directly or indirectly.

Players

The importance of players is obvious. They are at the center of any sport. Without them, there would be nothing for spectators to watch. If players are not skilled or committed enough, they will not become champions, or their teams will lose.

In 2009 Portuguese soccer player Cristiano Ronaldo became the most expensive soccer player in history, when the Spanish team Real Madrid paid around $120 million to buy him from the English team Manchester United. Real Madrid hoped that Ronaldo would bring success on the field, while also attracting fans from around the world to buy T-shirts and other merchandise.[1]

Spectators and fans

The other people that professional sports rely on are those who watch the sports, whether in person in a stadium or on television. As we have seen, professional leagues could only grow once there were enough people prepared to pay to watch the sports.

Spectators might buy tickets directly. Spectators and fans are also important to sponsors and advertisers. If millions of people are going to watch a particular sporting event, that means it creates a very powerful opportunity to place advertisements and create awareness of **brands** or services.

Owners and managers

In between these two essential parts of any professional sport are the people who actually own the clubs or pay the players. In individual sports such as tennis and golf, these people are the organizations that set up tournaments around the world.

Owners and managers of sports teams are often involved in sports for a variety of reasons. Some are involved because they love sports or because they want to give something back to their local community. Their main goal is to create a winning team. At the other end of the scale are people who see sports as a great way to make money. Their goal is to keep the fans happy, while also making as much money as possible.

Although these owners like to think of themselves as the most powerful people in sports, they need the support of players and fans to do their jobs. Fans can have enormous power if they get together, but because there are so many of them, this can be difficult.

BALANCING DIFFERENT INTERESTS

Some of the most powerful people in U.S. sports are the **commissioners**. These people are responsible for managing their sport as a whole and for working with owners, players, and others to safeguard the best interests of the sport. Often, the interests of these different groups are directly opposed. For example, owners would like to pay the players less, but the players are unlikely to want the same thing. A Major League Baseball (MLB) commissioner was first appointed after the "Black Sox" scandal of 1919, when Chicago White Sox players took **bribes** to lose the World Series.

Team support

There are many other people directly involved in the spectacle of sports, from team managers and coaches to physical therapists who keep the players in shape to play. There are also many other people who make their money from sports.

Agents

Agents normally represent the interests of athletes. Athletes' jobs are to be good at sports, and they are often eager to have someone else manage the business side of their career. Agents take a percentage of all the money that a player earns and negotiate contracts and salaries for the athlete. The more money agents make for an athlete, the more they will earn themselves. Critics of the role of agents say that they encourage players to be too concerned about money by always looking for the next deal. Agents argue that they are just doing the best they can to prevent their athletes from being paid less than they are worth.

MARK McCORMACK (1930–2003)

Mark McCormack has been called the "godfather of sports **marketing**." After training as a lawyer, McCormack became the agent for some of the world's most famous athletes. He was one of the first people to realize that sports stars were a great way for companies to advertise to the public, and that this could make a lot of money for those stars. In 1960 his IMG company signed its first client, golfer Arnold Palmer. The company went on to manage tennis stars, including Venus and Serena Williams.[2]

Media interest

It is no accident that the growth of professional sports has happened at the same time as the growth of the mass media. Sports organizations are eager to have their sport shown on television and covered in other media. Television companies know that sports will attract people to watch their channels. Many television companies would not exist without sports. There are also many journalists and technicians whose jobs depend on covering sports.

However, sports also rely on the media. The huge cost of staging the Olympic Games, the world's greatest sporting event, is only made possible because television companies will pay a lot of money to be able to show the Games. Sports leagues such as the National Football League (NFL) need to agree to big deals with television companies to pay the salaries that players and their agents expect.

Advertising and sponsorship

In addition to the television companies, there are the people who work in **advertising** and sponsorship. They are trying to sell products to people, and sports give them that opportunity. There are lots of people who watch sports, admire athletes, and will buy products associated with them (see pages 26–29). Once again, it all comes back to the sports fans.

Sportswear companies are an obvious type of business to use top athletes in their ads. Advertisers think their products will benefit from being associated with athletic success.

LIVING THE DREAM

Many sports fans dream of being like their sports heroes. As they play sports at school or in the park, they may imagine that they are hitting the winning run in the World Series or catching the final touchdown pass in the Super Bowl. These dreams are probably about the glory of sporting success or the roar of an approving crowd. Most of them are not about getting paid lots of money—even though that can be part of being a top athlete.

For most of us, these are just dreams. Some people will be good enough to play sports for their high school and then their college. The very best may even go on to be involved in professional sports at some level. For a tiny percentage of those boys and girls who dream of becoming a sports hero, the dream will become a reality.

Earning power

Sports are based on talent. Teams containing the best players will win trophies and attract fans. In individual sports such as tennis and golf, spectators and television viewers want to see the very best players. Attracting the top talents costs money, which is why the biggest stars are paid so much.

Many players in top team sports are paid a lot of money by their teams. However, there are many other ways for athletes to earn money.

- *Appearance money*: Athletes will often get paid every time they agree to appear to represent their team or play in a tournament.

- *Prize money*: Prizes for winning top tournaments in tennis and golf can be huge. The women's and men's U.S. Open tennis champions each take home slightly less than $2 million.[1]

- **Endorsements**: The very richest stars earn most of their money from contracts to **endorse** products. For example, Russian tennis star Maria Sharapova earned $24.5 million in 2010, but only $1 million came from prize money. Most of the rest was from contracts to promote various companies, including Nike and Sony.[2]

Do you think it is right that sports stars can earn so much money? Can it be justified that an athlete, no matter how talented, could earn more in a week than a firefighter or doctor does in a year?

THE WORLD'S HIGHEST-PAID SPORTS STARS

According to *Forbes* magazine, the world's highest-paid sports stars in 2010 were as follows[3]:

1. Tiger Woods (American, golf): $105 million
2. Floyd Mayweather (American, boxing): $65 million
3. Kobe Bryant (American, basketball): $48 million
4. Phil Mickelson (American, golf): $46 million
5. David Beckham (British, soccer): $43.7 million

The highest-paid female athlete in 2010 was tennis player Maria Sharapova, who earned $24.5 million.[4]

Average annual player earnings in major world sports leagues

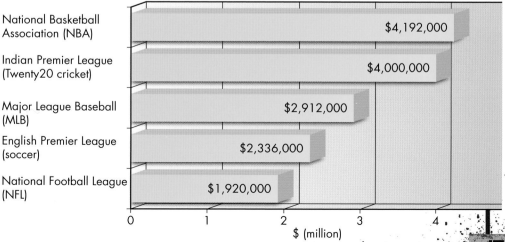

National Basketball Association (NBA)	$4,192,000
Indian Premier League (Twenty20 cricket)	$4,000,000
Major League Baseball (MLB)	$2,912,000
English Premier League (soccer)	$2,336,000
National Football League (NFL)	$1,920,000

$ (million)

Justifying player earnings

Is it possible to justify the huge amounts of money that a few athletes get paid? In most areas of business, there are a few people who earn much more than the average. These people often have skills that others don't have—and this is certainly true of star athletes. Sports are also all about entertainment, and star players create excitement and fun for viewers. Yet people are often more likely to question whether an athlete is paid too much than they are to question the money earned by a musician or movie star.

Athletes argue that they have a very short career. In most professional sports, players retire by their mid-30s. The career can be even shorter if they have to retire early due to injury. Players have to earn what they can when they are young, since it can be difficult for them to find other careers after they retire from playing sports.

Opponents would argue that star players and their agents receive too much of the money that comes into sports. They would argue that paying players means that less money goes to less glamorous areas of sports, such as encouraging sports at grass-roots levels, and less-wealthy fans have to pay too much to watch their favorite sports.

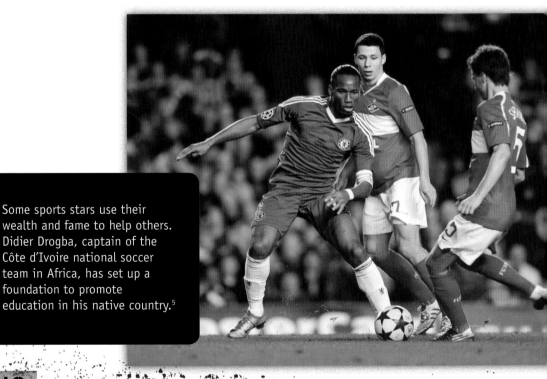

Some sports stars use their wealth and fame to help others. Didier Drogba, captain of the Côte d'Ivoire national soccer team in Africa, has set up a foundation to promote education in his native country.[5]

How does money affect athletes?

There is big money at stake in professional sports. This can put huge pressure on young athletes, many of whom do not come from wealthy backgrounds. These young stars may have had few opportunities to get an education, as their teenage years were spent striving to get to the top of their sports. They are then given more money than most young people could dream of. The media expect them to set an example for other young people because they are famous. Is this fair?

Yet many people would argue that athletes who are paid so much money have a duty to act responsibly. Millions of young people want to be like them. These people pay to watch them play, and that is partly why they are paid so well. On the other hand, we should not be surprised that athletes in this position occasionally make mistakes.

Some people also argue that top athletes are paid to play sports, so what they do in their private lives should make no difference.

WAYNE ROONEY (1985–)

English soccer star Wayne Rooney is one of the biggest names in soccer. According to press reports, he is paid as much as $300,000 per week[6] playing for the English soccer team Manchester United. He also earns millions from endorsements. Rooney comes from a working-class family in a tough area of Liverpool, England. He signed for a youth team at the age of 11 and was still a teenager when he joined Manchester United.

Rooney's skills have made him rich, but he has also been the subject of many press stories about his private life. Rooney's life changed dramatically at a very young age. Like many athletes, he has not always found it easy to adjust, and there was little in his background to prepare him for the demands of fame.[7]

Who gets paid the most?

Of course, the very best players earn much more than many of their teammates, particularly when endorsements are included. Why do some athletes earn so much more than others?

Sports are one area of life where it is relatively easy to measure success. In individual sports, the top earners are usually the ones who win the most often. In team sports, the value of a player could be decided by statistics, such as a baseball player's batting average.

Formula One racing drivers are some of the highest-paid sports people. Critics question whether championships are won by the best driver or whether success is due to having the best car.

But success cannot always be measured in points and statistics. Some players achieve popularity through skill and personality. They become popular with fans and valuable to their teams because of that skill, but also because fans identify with them.

The best players are very difficult or even impossible to replace. This means that owners of teams or people who organize tournaments are happy to pay more to make those athletes compete for them. Advertising works in the same way. Advertisers want the most recognizable and admired athletes to promote their products, and there are only a few of these top names.

Equal pay for women

In many sports, men are usually paid more than women. For years, this was the situation in tennis. Those who supported this situation argued that women's tennis was slower and less exciting than the men's game, so the prize money was lower. Opponents to this way of thinking said the best female players were just as fit as the men and were the best in their sport, so they should be rewarded in the same way. Today, prize money for men and women is equal in most major tennis tournaments. There are still many sports in which men are more highly paid, while the best women athletes are paid much less—if at all.

All sports are not equal

For every millionaire football player or basketball star, there are elite athletes in many sports who do not earn a lot of money. Athletes in many Olympic sports are now professionals, but they cannot hope to earn as much as the top stars in other sports. If these athletes are lucky, they may get financial support to help them train for the Olympics or a similar competition. To become champions at the Olympics or **Paralympics**, athletes have to train at least as hard, and show just as much skill, as stars of team sports. After all, only one athlete can win the Olympic gold medal.

The Paralympics, for athletes with disabilities, have grown in recent years. However, there is little money in Paralympic sports. These athletes are motivated by a love of their sport and a will to win.

The difference between the riches available in some sports compared to others shows that talent is not enough on its own. Sports such as football and basketball can afford to pay high salaries because thousands of people watch these sports every week, with millions more watching on television. In contrast, Olympic rowers or swimmers are supremely fit, but their sports do not generate the same money from television coverage and sponsorship.

TEAM OR FRANCHISE?

In team sports, spectators pay money to see one team play another. If you follow team sports, you probably support a team such as the New York Yankees or Chicago Bulls. Players, coaches, and even owners come and go, but these teams continue.

Many of the teams we know today were first set up as teams by a group of members. Often these were people who worked together in a particular **industry**. As more money came into sports and players became professionals, many teams became more like businesses. To be successful, teams have to play other teams. They are organized into leagues, and much of the money that comes into a sport goes to the league.

The power of leagues and clubs

In major sports such as football and baseball, the leagues are very powerful. The NFL was formed in 1920, with teams from across the Midwest. By 1933 the league was made up mostly of teams called **franchises** from different cities across the country.[1] The league has changed and expanded as new franchises have been added, particularly in cities that have grown in recent decades, such as those in the southwestern part of the United States. Sometimes franchises have moved to different cities.

In other sports, particularly international soccer, most of the power is with individual clubs, or teams. Although clubs play together in a league, they have traditionally been very much a part of the local area. Today, however, foreign owners have bought many teams, and star players come from around the world (see pages 32–33). Exceptions to this rule include Barcelona, one of the biggest and most successful soccer clubs of all. It is still owned by its fans and is seen by many as the national team of the Catalonia region of Spain.

Who are modern sports franchises for?

When the first modern sports teams were formed, they were formed by players and fans. In the 2000s, teams have much more money. But many fans question whether the teams are still run for them. Do they exist as a service to the community? Or are sports teams really just there to enrich their owners, who may live thousands of miles away? To find the answers, we need to look more closely at who owns the top sports teams.

BIG MONEY IN CRICKET

Cricket was created in England, but the center of the cricket world is increasingly becoming India, with millions of fanatical fans. In 2008 a new league changed world cricket forever. This league was created to play a game called Twenty20 cricket, which was first played in England in 2003. This shortened form of the game only lasts around three hours, rather than the whole day or more for other forms of cricket.[2] The eight new franchises in the league, representing Indian cities such as Mumbai and Kolkata, were funded by some of India's biggest **corporations**. Money was at the heart of the venture, with television **rights** sold for $1 billion. Top players were paid up to $1.5 million to play for six weeks in the Indian Premier League (IPL).[3]

In 2009 the IPL was threatened by concerns about security. Organizers decided to hold the tournament in South Africa. Fans in India and around the world could still watch on TV and big money could be made from TV rights and advertising.

Heart and head

It takes a lot of money to run a successful sports team. Businesspeople who get involved because they love sports may find that they make some decisions with their heart rather than their head. They may spend more money on player salaries than they can afford, in order to beat their rivals.

Who owns your team?

Who owns your favorite team? Do the owners come to watch every game, or have they never seen the team play? You may feel that these questions are not important, as long as the team keeps winning. However, if the team is just another investment for the owners, they may not be too concerned about the success of the team—as long as they can make money from it. However, winning and making money often go together.

Should we really expect the owners of sports teams to be any different from any other business owners? One key difference is in the connection between sports teams and their fans. Many businesses have shareholders who are concerned about making profits, but sports fans are unlikely to boast about the money their team makes. Rather, fans have an emotional link to their team and are loyal.

Making money in sports

Owners can make money from their team in many different ways. They can sell tickets for people to watch games. As we have seen, television and sponsorships can also generate a lot of money in many sports.

The NFL works on the principle that the league will be more popular if all the teams are strong. Money made from television is divided equally, so all teams benefit from the huge television audiences for the sport. This, along with a limit on what teams can spend on salaries, means that any team can go on to win the Super Bowl.

This is very different from the situation in international soccer. In Spain, the two biggest soccer teams, Real Madrid and Barcelona, can make their own television deals. Because of the money from these deals, these clubs can afford to pay more for the best players. So more often than not, they are the best teams.

Although teams in the English **Premier League** share television money, bigger stadiums and sales of branded merchandise mean that some teams have more money than others. In leagues where some teams have much more money, the richer teams can come to dominate the league, since they can afford all the best players.

UNITED DIVIDED

The Glazer family (pictured above) bought the English soccer team Manchester United in 2005. Manchester United had become a public company, meaning that anyone could buy a piece of the company. This move was planned to raise more money from investors. But when the Glazers tried to buy all the shares at once, there was little that people who opposed the move could do about it.[4] Fans believe that the Glazers have made big profits while loading huge debts on the club.

SPONSORS, ENDORSEMENTS, AND THE MEDIA

We know that professional sports would not exist without fans and spectators. In addition to paying to watch sports, fans are also the reason why other corporations want to put money into sports.

Corporate sponsors are a part of most sports. Some are directly linked to the sports, such as sportswear or equipment companies. Others have little connection to sports, such as restaurants and soft drinks.

Everything in sports gets sponsored, from shirts and sunglasses to stadiums. Renaming the stadium after a sponsor means that the sponsor's name gets mentioned every time the stadium is talked about. Sportswear companies compete as hard as the teams themselves to win the right to make the shirts for the biggest leagues and the best teams. In motor sports such as NASCAR and Formula One, drivers' suits and cars are covered in company names and **logos**.

Athletes in individual sports, including tennis and golf, can choose what they wear themselves. For a sportswear company to get their shirts, caps, and equipment in the hands of the top players can mean huge exposure on television. As players like Tiger Woods and Venus and Serena Williams have discovered, this means that the company will pay many millions for the privilege to have a star wear their brand.

What's in it for the sponsor?

There are lots of other ways for companies to get their message across. They could advertise on television in the commercial breaks between programs— but viewers might flip around the channels and miss their advertisement. Putting the right brand of shirt on an athlete means that viewers cannot help but see it. Moreover, the brand gets associated with success.

TIGER WOODS (1975–)

Eldrick "Tiger" Woods has changed the sport of golf forever. He has also changed the business of sports, as his earnings from golf and endorsements are regularly more than $100 million per year. Woods won his first major title in 1997, at the age of 21. Many more followed, and he is close to winning a record number of major titles. As a young mixed-race athlete in a sport dominated by older white people, Woods brought golf to a whole new part of the population. This made him a perfect athlete for corporate sponsors.

From 2009 Woods's dominance of golf was affected by injuries. Stories about his private life also damaged his clean-cut image, leading to the loss of some of his endorsements. Still, Woods remains one of the hottest properties in sports.[1]

If people are going to buy a pair of sneakers, they are more likely to choose ones that are associated with top athletes, such as basketball stars, even if they cost a little more. Many athletic gear companies have learned this lesson. Nike is one company that has built a very successful business out of its associations with stars such as Serena Williams and basketball legend Michael Jordan.

Away from the bright lights

Sponsorship of sports is not just about paying millions to the biggest stars. Many athletes in amateur sports or smaller-scale sports benefit from sponsors who give them enough money to keep training or give up work for sports. Sports teams can also benefit from small deals with local businesses, which help the team to keep going.

Problems with endorsements

Not everyone thinks the amount of **commercial** sponsorship that takes place in sports is a good thing. They point out that the millions of dollars in endorsements paid to top stars have to come from somewhere. A pair of sneakers that costs more than $150 does not cost that much to make. The company knows that people will pay more because of the link to their favorite sports star. The higher price tag also means that the company can afford to pay millions of dollars in endorsements and advertising.

Sportswear company Nike pays basketball star Kobe Bryant millions of dollars to wear the shoes that carry his name.

Bad influence

Some people believe that sports sponsorship and promotion is much more likely to influence people than regular advertising, because people associate brands with sports heroes. This is what the brands are trying to do. But do they have too much influence on what we buy? This could be an even bigger problem if associating a product with sports makes it seem healthy when it is not (see the box on the next page).

Promoting a healthy lifestyle

Hopefully, the examples set by our sports heroes will encourage us to take part in sports. Playing sports and exercising is part of a healthy lifestyle. But not all the products that are advertised or endorsed by athletes and sporting events are part of a healthy lifestyle. In the past, sporting events were even sponsored by deadly tobacco products. Sponsors of the 2012 Olympic Games include Coca-Cola and McDonalds[2], which are not healthy when compared to other food and drink.

Opponents of sponsorship also argue that it takes away from the values of sports. The Olympic Movement prides itself on involving people from every nation on Earth. Yet the Olympic Games are partly funded by a small group of very powerful corporations, mostly based in Europe and North America, from sportswear to oil companies. Without these companies, the burden of paying for the Olympics and similar events would be on those who buy tickets and on the general public through taxes.

Extreme sponsorship

For some sports outside the mainstream, sponsorship is a major route to success. In sports such as skateboarding and snowboarding, young people may be able to get free or reduced-price equipment that helps them to develop their skills—in return for promoting the manufacturer. Top riders are paid by manufacturers to appear at events around the world.[3] Do you think this is a good way to fund street sports? Or does it just make them another branch of advertising?

CRICKET CIRCUS

Sometimes sports sponsors may not be all that they seem to be. In 2008 Texan billionaire Allen Stanford landed his helicopter on Lord's Cricket Ground in London, England, and offered $20 million to the winners of a Twenty20 cricket match between England and the West Indies. However, Stanford's millions were not based on firm foundations. Within a year, Stanford's business empire had collapsed, and he was in jail facing charges of fraud. Many people had lost their savings in the scandal, particularly on the Caribbean island of Antigua.[4]

Television and media money

Perhaps the greatest influence of all on sports is television. Television companies such as ESPN have been built on the idea of persuading people to pay extra for cable television to watch sports. Television has been seen as the main reason for the riches now available to players in leagues such as the NFL, NBA, and English Premier League soccer.

"The most watched events in history, by some margin, are the opening ceremony of the Olympics Games and the [soccer] World Cup final. Historical events, like the inauguration of Barack Obama or the funeral of Princess Diana . . . simply don't have the same scale of television audiences that mass sports events can generate."[5]

Kevin Alavy, television sports expert

Television coverage of sports is probably better than it has ever been. Cable and satellite channels provide sports coverage 24 hours every day from around the world. But can this be a problem?

One thing that people complain about is that television has too much influence over the sports themselves. U.S. television networks pay large sums for the television rights to show the Olympic Games. Olympic organizers have been accused in the past of giving in to pressure to rearrange events to suit peak viewing times in the United States.[6] Television has also had an influence on how and when games are played, with pauses for advertising in some sports breaking up the game. On the other hand, if television companies are paying for the sports to be staged, why shouldn't they have some influence?

Women and televised sports

Televised sports are designed to appeal to a particular audience. Television companies sell advertising to companies based on who they believe will be watching. This can mean that television networks only focus on the most popular and high-profile sports—which will, in turn, attract the most high-paying advertisers. One area that suffers is sports for women. Women's tennis is one of the only sports that gets a similar amount of coverage as the men's game, yet almost as many women as men play competitive sports.

Paying extra

Television companies have figured out that viewers will often pay extra to watch sports on television. This means that many sports are now shown only on cable or satellite television, so people have to pay for the service. If sports are not accessible to young people on free television, some people fear that fewer people will become interested in sports, as the example of boxing shows (see the box below).

The decline of boxing

Many major boxing matches are televised on pay-per-view cable television, meaning that viewers have to pay a fee for each match, even if it only lasts a few minutes. This has meant that top boxers can earn more money than ever before. Despite this, the popularity of boxing has declined. Pay-per-view television means that the sports they show are failing to attract new fans. There are also several different organizations, each signed to different television channels, that each claim they have a world champion.

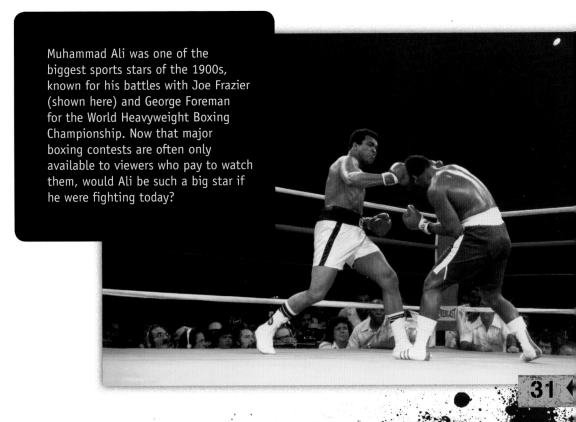

Muhammad Ali was one of the biggest sports stars of the 1900s, known for his battles with Joe Frazier (shown here) and George Foreman for the World Heavyweight Boxing Championship. Now that major boxing contests are often only available to viewers who pay to watch them, would Ali be such a big star if he were fighting today?

Other media

Television is not the only medium to rely on sports. Before television was invented, people bought newspapers for sports reports and listened to games on the radio. Sports reporting and commentary is still an important part of newspapers and news websites. But the Internet has meant that there are many more places for sports to be covered than ever before.

These different media outlets also play a big part in spreading sports brands around the world. The Internet and live television mean that there are fans of teams such as the New York Yankees across the world.

Global brands

The days when sports teams were made up of only local players and fans have long gone. Teams in many sports are now made up of athletes from many different countries.

Teams and leagues have also tried to find fans around the world and build themselves into global brands. The NFL stages a football game every year in London's Wembley Stadium to build support in Europe. Premier League soccer teams regularly play matches in North America and particularly in Asia. Formula One race car driving has also staged events in Arab and Asian countries, including China. Some of these ventures have been successful, particularly if local athletes are part of the international teams—for example, a Chinese basketball player or Korean soccer player.

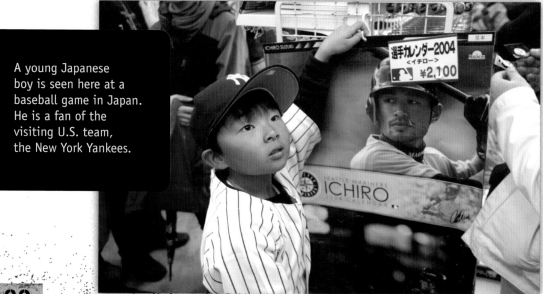

A young Japanese boy is seen here at a baseball game in Japan. He is a fan of the visiting U.S. team, the New York Yankees.

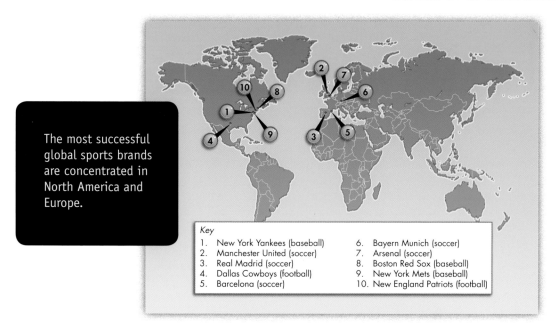

The most successful global sports brands are concentrated in North America and Europe.

Key
1. New York Yankees (baseball)
2. Manchester United (soccer)
3. Real Madrid (soccer)
4. Dallas Cowboys (football)
5. Barcelona (soccer)
6. Bayern Munich (soccer)
7. Arsenal (soccer)
8. Boston Red Sox (baseball)
9. New York Mets (baseball)
10. New England Patriots (football)

Having fans around the world brings sports teams lots of money. These fans may watch games on television and buy shirts and other merchandise. However, many people believe that these global brands have become too distant from their roots as local teams. Sports teams have traditionally been part of local cultures, but this might not be the case if players, fans, and owners can live anywhere in the world. Also, if people in Shanghai, China, or Cape Town, South Africa, are supporting teams in North America or Europe, that also might mean that they will not be helping to develop teams in their local areas.

World tours

In individual sports such as tennis and golf, players already compete on a schedule of tournaments around the world. Tennis and golf have a few tournaments each year that are considered the major competitions, but the schedule changes and these major, or "Grand Slam," tournaments are no longer the best-paying prizes on the circuit. Will money start to dictate which competitions are the most important to athletes?

Local or global?

Do you support a local team or one in another city or country? Your view about sports teams as global brands probably affects your answer to that question. If you support a local team, you may feel you have more of a connection to your team than friends who support one of the bigger teams.

FANS AND FOLLOWERS

We traditionally think of fans as the people sitting in the stadium. But today, fans are just as likely to be sitting in front of a television or computer screen, possibly on another continent. In all the media reports about player salaries and huge television deals, it is easy to forget that none of this would happen without fans.

The teams and athletes that attract big sponsorship deals are the ones that already have the most fans and win the most trophies. Fans of the biggest teams and best athletes also generally have to pay more to watch their team. This means that the rich get even richer.

Fan loyalty

In other areas of business, customers come and go. People might buy food, clothes, or other goods in the cheapest or most convenient place they can find. The Internet allows people to compare prices and services instantly. It is little wonder that many businesses complain that customers are not loyal. Yet, as we have seen, sports teams rarely have this problem. Once people have chosen which team to support, they do not usually change.

Do owners take advantage of this loyalty? Many of them certainly try to make money out of it. **Replica** team jerseys are sometimes redesigned every year so that the "true fan" will have to buy a new one. Yet sportswear companies would argue that no one is forced to buy merchandise.

THE COST OF WATCHING SPORTS

Following the top teams can cost a lot of money. In the NBA, the highest ticket prices are almost $100, although many teams have cut prices. The average cost of taking a family of four to an NBA game in 2010—including four tickets, four hot dogs, beverages, parking, two game programs, and two caps—was $290. That does not include the cost of jerseys or other merchandise.[1]

It costs hundreds of dollars for a family to attend an NFL game. In recent years, the number of people attending games has fallen slightly, and organizers are concerned that people are choosing to watch games on television instead.[2]

The loyalty of fans contrasts with the behavior of some owners and players, who regularly switch between different teams. The athlete who spends an entire career with one team used to be quite common, but it is increasingly rare today. This is partly because athletes now have more freedom to move.

In 2010 basketball star LeBron James shocked fans when he moved from the Cleveland Cavaliers, where he had been a huge favorite, to the Miami Heat. Cleveland fans felt betrayed by their local hero.[3]

LeBron James announced his decision to join the Miami Heat in an hour-long TV special.

What do fans want?

Although fans may feel betrayed when their favorite player leaves, they will probably soon find a new hero. Even the most loyal athletes will often only be with a team for a few years. So what else is important to a team's fans?

The most important thing is to have a winning team. In any sport, there are only a few trophies to win, and these often seem to be won by a small group of teams. So at any one time, most fans feel that their team should be more successful. Since the fans are mainly concerned with success, they will ask for more money to be spent on players. But some sports, such as basketball, impose a salary cap. This means that no single team can pay more than the others to attract all the best players.

"Nice to see your home fans boo you, that's loyal fans."[4]

English soccer star Wayne Rooney's comment on how fans reacted to his team's disappointing performance during the 2010 soccer World Cup finals. Many fans had traveled thousands of miles and spent their savings to watch the team play in South Africa.

Fans also want to feel as if they are a part of their team. Although success is important, fans often show huge loyalty to their teams, even if the team has not won a championship for many years.

Owners need fans

Owners need fans for more than just the money they pay for tickets. A full stadium and a cheering crowd is an essential part of the television spectacle that is beamed around the world. Sports organizers have desperately tried to fill empty seats when they have appeared in high-profile events such as the Olympics or the World Cup.[5]

Many of the great sports rivalries exist where there are two teams in one city, such as the Chicago Cubs and White Sox baseball teams. But for money managers in sports, it often makes sense to have only one team in each city. That way, the team will be supported by everyone in that city. However, for the local fan, the rivalry with friends and coworkers who support the other team in the city can be very important. Sometimes teams have moved to different cities where there is no team, in order to tap into a new "market."

Fans of national sporting teams will often spend money and time supporting their team around the world. These Dutch fans are dressed in the orange shirts of the Netherlands soccer team at the 2010 soccer World Cup in South Africa.

Corporate guests

We have already seen that sponsors provide much of the money that goes into sports. Sponsors of teams and major tournaments will often be given tickets to entertain people who they do business with or who work for the company. For popular events, these corporate guests, who may only have a passing interest in the sport itself, take up valuable tickets that could have gone to real fans. Despite this, many new stadiums are built to accommodate more corporate guests, often with private "VIP" boxes. These corporate guests are treated well. because they bring in more money than regular fans.

THE STARS OF TOMORROW

Winning a championship once is great for any team. Owners know that they can attract the biggest stars if they are regularly competing for big prizes at the end of the season. One way to create lasting success is to find the stars of the future.

College players

In the United States, colleges have always been important in the development of amateur sports. Today, they still have a big role in professional sports through the **National Collegiate Athletic Association (NCAA)**. College teams have become a training ground for the athletes who may go on to earn millions in professional sports. Every year, the best college football and basketball players are **drafted** by professional teams. College sports are very popular in their own right, with games shown live on television and big fees paid by television companies to show the sports.

SHOULD COLLEGE ATHLETES BE AMATEUR?

The NCAA receives more than $500 million for the television rights to college basketball,[1] but the players are all amateur until they sign with professional teams. Big money is being made from college sports, but the players do not share in the profits. Those who think this is fair argue that college athletes normally have their college tuition paid through a scholarship, and that college sports programs are very expensive to run. However, as the appeal of college sports grows, calls for players to be paid are growing louder and louder.

John Wall was spotted as a future basketball star while he was still at school. After three successful years at the University of Kentucky, Wall was the number one pick in the NBA draft for 2009–10, when he joined the Washington Wizards.

Although basketball and football get more exposure than other college sports, they are not the only professional sports that draft athletes from colleges. In 2009, Women's Professional Soccer (WPS) was launched in the United States, with all-important television coverage. WPS attracts players from around the world. There are plans to launch other professional soccer leagues for women in other countries.

Money and future stars

Finding the best young talent is also about money. In international soccer, soccer teams often develop their own young players. That way, they don't have to pay quite so much in large fees (called transfer fees) and salaries to bring players in from other teams.

Smaller teams see it very differently. If they can find and coach young players, they can "sell" them to bigger teams and make money on the deal. Smaller teams do not benefit from big television deals and fans buying shirts in China. Rather, they rely on selling players to keep the team going. Teams from the wealthy leagues of Europe often invest in soccer players from Africa and South America, in the hopes of making them the next global stars.

Too much, too young

It is very tough to get accepted into the college sports system, and the pressure to succeed is intense. However, it does protect young athletes from the huge pressures of professional sports. Some would argue that young athletes do not need this protection. After all, young people who want to succeed in other areas where chances of success are small, such as acting or art, do not get the same kind of protection.

Still, some athletes are encouraged to sign with a professional team without going to college. Young tennis players train in tennis camps far away from home, and there are many examples of teenage tennis stars who have lost their love of the game or experienced problems in later life.

MARTINA HINGIS (1980–)

Swiss tennis star Martina Hingis (seen below at a tournament in France in 1995) started playing tennis at the age of three. Hingis turned professional just after her 14th birthday. In 1997, at just 16 years old, she won the Australian Open, the youngest player since 1887 to win a Grand Slam tournament, and she reached the top of the world rankings. She won four more Grand Slam events, including Wimbledon and U.S. Open titles in 1997—at a time in her life when many young people would have been preparing for college.[2]

After an amazing career as a teenager, Hingis suffered from a series of injuries. She retired in 2007, after testing positive for cocaine at the Wimbledon championships. Hingis denied taking drugs but said that, at 27, she was "too old to play top-class tennis."[3] Since Hingis's debut, women's tennis has changed its rules to prevent 14-year-olds from playing in major tournaments, and it has limited the amount of tennis 15- to 17-year-olds can play.[4]

Fear of failure

In international soccer, players are identified and signed up by teams as early as possible. Individual teams control their own training academies and are desperate to sign the best players before their rivals. Although players cannot officially sign a contract until they are 16, there are other ways to make sure they sign with a team. Big teams have been accused of offering parents jobs or money to ensure that their children sign on the dotted line as soon as they turn 16. But, at age 18, these young players can be dropped from their contracts.

"I was quite fortunate because I got a contract early, but I'll never forget the day the rest of the boys found out [that they wouldn't get contracts]. One by one they had to go in and see the manager . . . I know people always say [soccer players] have got a great life, and they're right. But to get there is so tough."[5]

Young soccer player Chris Gunter remembers the anxious wait to find out if he would be given a contract

There are many questions about whether some of the systems of finding new talent are really the best thing for young athletes. Young people often give up their education for the promise of huge salaries. However, many of them do not make it big, and they end up with little to fall back on. More often than not, the chance that everyone dreams of ends in disappointment.

The lucky few who make it to the top in professional sports may be able to earn big money, but they are not immune from the pressures that top-level sports put on young bodies. Their careers may be cut short by injury because of too much training at a young age. Many young stars also find it difficult to deal with the pressures of their newfound wealth and fame.

SPORTS FOR EVERYONE

This book has focused on the impact of money on the most popular professional sports, where the money involved is often counted in millions and even billions. However, the top professional leagues are just the most visible part of the world of sports. Not everyone who plays sports earns a lot of money or is internationally recognized. Still, money often plays a role in this smaller-scale world of sports.

Lower down the ladder

In sports leagues such as Major League Baseball (MLB) and Premier League soccer, some money goes to training and building the skills of younger players. But many people feel that too much money goes to the lucky few in the major leagues instead.

Minor League Baseball, which feeds players to the Major League teams, has seen bigger crowds in recent years.[1] Lower-league soccer teams attract millions of people every weekend, yet they receive a fraction of the money from television and sponsors compared to the top leagues. If a bigger and bigger share of the money in sports goes to the top leagues, popular teams in lower leagues could decline. Yet some people point out that more exposure for a sport benefits the whole sport, even if it is concentrated in the top leagues.

Around the world

Outside of the **developed countries** that dominate the business of sports, the flow of money to local sports is even more important. Major teams and leagues in North America and Europe want to establish themselves as global brands around the world. If much of the interest and money of sports fans in Southeast Asia or the Caribbean is going to NBA teams or Premier League soccer, that may mean that leagues and teams don't develop in those countries. On the other hand, increasing the popularity of these sports in different parts of the world could lead to new leagues developing or local athletes choosing to take up the sports.

The dominance of big-money sports can affect local sports. For example, in the 1970s and 1980s, the Caribbean had the most feared and respected team in world cricket. Its talented players were heroes around the world. In recent years, young people in the Caribbean have become more likely to play basketball or soccer, attracted by television coverage of the NBA and English Premier League. This has led to a decline in a sport that is part of the culture of the region. Although fans of Caribbean cricket see this as a bad thing, young people in the region may benefit from being exposed to a wider range of sports.

MONEY FOR OLYMPIC ATHLETES

Although Olympic athletes may compete in tournaments regularly, their main goal is to reach their peak every four years for the Summer or Winter Olympic Games. Athletes have to support themselves for four years, particularly in sports that have less media coverage.

Olympic athletes are supported financially in many ways. Money may come from the government or from private and corporate sponsorship. Colleges also provide lots of support for Olympic athletes.

Winning gold medals at the Olympics is important for many countries. To achieve this, they have to make sure that Olympic athletes get enough money to train full-time.

Sports for fun and exercise

Millions of people play sports for fun and exercise. These people earn no money from sports, but money still affects the sports they play.

Sports are bigger business than ever, but people in many developed countries have never been more unfit. This is because the typical diet is less healthy than it has been in the past. Western lifestyles also involve little exercise, as people spend much of their time in front of a computer screen or the television. This combination of factors leads to serious health problems for many people.

Do televised sports do enough to encourage people to take up exercise? When London was bidding to host the 2012 Olympics, one of the main features of the bid was a wish to inspire young people to take up sports and provide facilities for them to do so.[2] Many sports businesses do work in their local communities, but the focus on using sports to sell things does not always recognize the importance of participating in sports. It can even send mixed messages when super-fit athletes promote unhealthy food and drinks.

Counting the cost

Sportswear and equipment companies pay big money to top stars to promote their goods. They also spend money advertising those goods. If you are one of those people who have to have the latest sneakers or jerseys, a big chunk of the money you hand over in the store is going into the pockets of star athletes. The clothing companies wouldn't pay the stars to wear their products if they couldn't make it back from their customers.

As we have seen, particular sports and teams get more media coverage. Other areas of sports, including less-popular sports and women's sports, can get overlooked in the waves of media coverage of the biggest sports. This can also contribute to turning some people away from sports.

Turning people off sports

There are also concerns that the focus on sport as a business changes the nature of sports. Young talented athletes see sports as a possible career, and this means that their focus is on winning and moving to the next level, rather than playing sports for fun. This focus on winning and building a career also deters people who might enjoy playing sports but are put off because they feel they are not good enough to compete.

Buying equipment

Money can affect the sports that people play, too. Sports such as skiing or ice hockey need expensive equipment and facilities. This limits whether people can afford to play them. Sports that need little or no equipment, such as running and soccer, attract athletes from a wide range of backgrounds, particularly in **developing countries**. African athletes from Ethiopia and Kenya have, for example, dominated middle-distance and long-distance running.

The world's most popular sport—soccer—requires not much more than a ball and a flat area to play on, as shown by these boys in Cape Town.

DIRTY MONEY

With so much money in sports, it is not just athletes who can become rich from them. Unfortunately, some people take shortcuts to make money out of sports by bending and breaking the rules.

The better athletes perform, the more money they make. Some athletes are tempted to illegally improve their performance by taking drugs that make them quicker or stronger, or that help them to recover more quickly from injury. These athletes risk lengthy bans, serious health problems, and, in some cases, prison if they get caught.

Many high-profile athletes have been caught taking performance-enhancing drugs in track and field sports. These accusations have also been made about athletes in other sports, including baseball. If some of the biggest hitters in baseball have used performance-enhancing drugs during their career, the drugs are at least partly responsible for the millions they have earned.

Money may also affect the way athletes play the game in general. Some people question whether the huge rewards that come from professional sports can change people's behavior, making them question refereeing decisions or not play as fairly as they would if there were no money involved.

STAGING MAJOR EVENTS

Staging the Olympics or the soccer World Cup is very expensive, but the bidders think it is worth the cost. London is expecting 320,000 visitors for the Olympic Games in 2012,[1] and the event will have a huge television audience around the world.

However, many people question whether these events give value for money. Sports venues built for the Olympics in Athens, Greece, have not been used since the Games were held there in 2004. London may even have fewer visitors than usual in 2012 due to high prices and security during the Olympics.[2]

Staging huge events like the Olympic Games brings the world's attention and prestige to a city. Beijing, China, probably staged the most expensive Olympics ever in 2008.

Corruption in sports

Some of the biggest prizes in sports are the sporting events themselves. Countries and cities compete for the chance to host the Olympic Games and the soccer World Cup. Host cities and countries believe they can make a lot of money from staging these events, although this is not always the case. Decisions about who will host these events are made by members of committees, such as the more than 100 members of the International Olympic Committee (IOC).

In 1999 six members of the IOC were expelled and four others resigned after the media discovered evidence that some IOC members were accepting bribes and gifts in exchange for their votes. The scandal was particularly centered on the bid by Salt Lake City, Utah, to stage the 2002 Winter Olympics. The IOC changed its rules to prevent this kind of scandal from happening again.[3] In 2010 the British media claimed that members of soccer's governing body, the International Federation of Football Association (FIFA), had also accepted gifts from countries trying to host the World Cup.

Gambling and sports

Betting and gambling have been part of amateur and professional sports for centuries. Gamblers bet money on the outcome of a race or game. If they bet correctly, they win more money. Betting is a major part of horse racing and is also widespread in football, soccer, and other team sports. Gamblers will often bet through **bookmakers**, who decide how likely a particular result is—and so how much the gambler will win. Online gambling has led to a big increase in betting on sports.

Gambling on sports is illegal in many countries. This is partly because gambling is forbidden by some religions, but also because gamblers can become addicted. This leads to crime and social problems, as gamblers may owe large amounts of money. Despite this, betting on many aspects of sports is big business.

Gambling and bookmaking rely on predicting what will happen in a contest. Large sums of money can be made by influencing the people actually involved in the event. This has happened in some sports, and it is another reason why betting on sports is restricted. The growth of online gambling makes this more difficult to monitor, however, as gambling crosses national boundaries.

Bribery and betting

In some cases, athletes themselves have become involved with gambling groups. Illegal betting on cricket matches is extremely popular in South Asia, and there have been accusations of players accepting money from bookmakers to influence the game.[4]

Those who want to fix games use clever tactics to lure players into helping them. At first, players might be paid to do something very minor that does not affect the outcome of a game. Once a player has done this, demands from bookmakers may get more serious, and the player is unable to refuse for fear of being found out. Still, a single team member can only have a limited influence on the outcome of a game. Gamblers have also targeted individual sports like horse racing.

Referees and umpires can also affect the outcome of a game. In 2010 a trial began in Germany suggesting widespread bribery of players and referees in some European soccer leagues. The scandal was discovered after a German referee was convicted of taking bribes to influence matches.[5]

THE "BLACK SOX" SCANDAL

One of the most infamous betting scandals in sports history affected the World Series, baseball's biggest event. Eight players from the Chicago White Sox were banned for life after admitting to deliberately losing the 1919 series against the Cincinnati Reds, in exchange for bribes from gamblers.[6] Following the "Black Sox" scandal, baseball appointed a commissioner to clean up the sport.

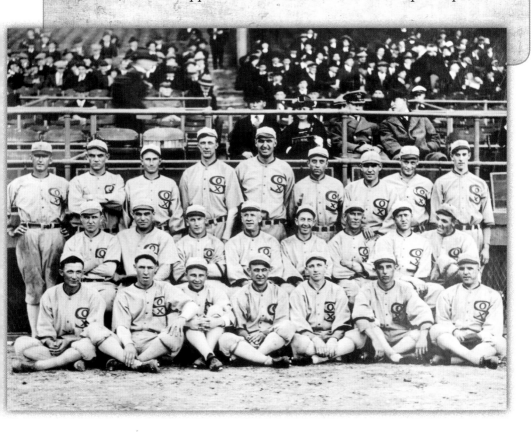

How betting scandals undermine sports

When you watch or play a sport, you have to believe certain things. You have to believe that everyone in the game is doing his or her best to win, and that any mistake they make happens by accident. Once a betting scandal is discovered in a sport, people start to question every game and performance. People cannot be passionate about sports if they do not believe in what they are seeing.

THE FUTURE OF SPORTS AND MONEY

Sports are becoming increasingly global. As we have read, most modern professional sports originated in the United States, Britain, or Europe. In the late 1800s, these countries were the world's economic powers. But in the 2000s, economic power is shifting to countries such as India and China, both of which are home to more than one billion people. China won more gold medals than any other nation at the Beijing Olympic Games in 2008, and huge interest in cricket in India has made it into one of the world's biggest sports. The spread of sports around the globe has given many people more opportunities to enjoy and take part in sports.

Sports can be truly global. David Beckham has used his success as a soccer player to become one of the most recognized people on the planet. In 2010 *Bend It Like Beckham*, a movie about a girl who wants to play soccer like her hero, was the first Western film to be shown on television in secretive North Korea.[1]

Money has also made sports into a major industry, providing work directly or indirectly for many thousands of people. The biggest stars in sports often come from poor backgrounds. Skill on the field or the court has made them famous and wealthy. It could be argued that people should celebrate their success, rather than criticize them for earning too much money. People should also remember that most of the individuals who work in sports are not earning huge amounts of money.

Fitter and faster

Professional athletes are fitter, faster, and more skilled than the athletes of the past. With so much competition in professional sports, they can't afford to be anything else. This is good for sports. Professional sports and money have also brought improvements in facilities and medical knowledge.

Television and the Internet also mean we can watch and enjoy more sports than ever before, including live sports from around the world. There may be some downsides to the relationship between money and sports, but many people—including television executives, sponsors, and the top teams and athletes—would argue that the world of sports has never been better than it is now.

THE SUPER BOWL

If you are in any doubt about the close relationship between sports and money, watch the Super Bowl. This is the climax to the NFL season, and it is as much about entertainment and **commerce** as it is about sports. Media coverage before the event focuses on which music stars will perform during the halftime show and the cost of advertising in the many commercial breaks—as well as on the teams who will take the field. The Super Bowl is held in a different city every year, and it is one of the most-watched events on television.[2]

In 2011, the Black Eyed Peas performed the halftime show at the Super Bowl in Arlington, Texas. Artists who perform at the Super Bowl often see an increase in sales of their music.

The case against commercialism

Not everyone is happy about the way that money is such a huge part of modern sports. These people point to the fact that media stories are as likely to talk about how much an athlete is being paid as they are about his or her performance in a game. The focus of money and media attention on the top stars of a few sports means that many true sporting heroes who excel in less popular sports or triumph over adversity are ignored. This particularly affects areas of sport that are seen as less valuable by TV companies and advertisers, including many women's sports.

The first sports teams were rooted in their local area. Players and spectators would live on the same street, and the local football or baseball team would be part of the area's identity. Some of these teams are now global businesses, with players, owners, and fans from all over the world.

While no one can deny that the industry of sport employs many people, critics point out that some of the most important people in sports are either ignored or treated solely as customers for tickets, shirts, and whatever else advertisers want to sell to them. They argue that teams and franchises should be run more for the benefit of loyal supporters.

Striking a balance

The truth probably lies somewhere between the two sides of the argument about money. Supporting professional sports gives many people a lot of enjoyment. Athletes who entertain millions of people deserve to be well paid just as much as top entertainers are. However, if money becomes too powerful, it can destroy the excitement, passion, and unpredictability that make sports worth following in the first place.

Back to the people

Playing sports regularly can help people to stay in good health. It can also help people learn how to work as a team and build lasting friendships. But in many places where these benefits are most needed, there are no facilities to encourage young people to take up sports. Many companies do put money into local projects. But a share of the money that goes to the top sports could make a difference in many communities.

THE RYDER CUP

Some of the biggest prizes in sports are not about money. Golf is one of the best-paying sports, with top players earning millions from prize money and endorsements. Yet the winners of one of golf's biggest events receive no money at all.

The Ryder Cup is held every two years between teams of golfers from the United States and Europe. Players compete for the honor of winning the cup, rather than any prize money. It is also one of the few events where golfers play as a team. Ironically, the organizations that arrange the Ryder Cup make lots of money from television rights, ticket sales, and corporate guests.[3]

The Ryder Cup was first held in 1927. Winning is about honor rather than money, although the teams are made up of golfers who have won the most prize money in other tournaments.

TOPICS FOR DISCUSSION

As this book shows, there are many arguments about the relationship between sports and money, and whether this is beneficial for sports.

Here are a few questions to consider:

- Many people believe that top-level sports are now all about money. Is this true? What arguments would you use for or against this idea? Remember that there are many more people involved in professional sports than just the players you see.

- What are the benefits of amateur and professional sports? What would happen if all sports were still amateur? Would they be as exciting as professional sports, and would standards of skill and fitness be as high?

- Do professional players earn too much money? What factors do you think decide a player's value? If you think they earn too much, how would you change sports to reduce players' salaries? Who should earn the most?

- Sportswear companies sponsor many sports teams and athletes. Does this persuade you to buy a particular brand of sportswear or shoes? How effective are endorsements by sports stars in persuading people to spend money?

- You could find out more about branded sportswear for your favorite team or athlete. Where is it made, and how much does it cost? Many top brands cost very little to produce, and there have been questions about conditions for workers in some factories. Does this fit with the image that these companies try to project through sports?

- Is money from television companies good for sports? There are more sports on television than ever before, but is this really good for the sports? Does the money paid by television benefit the whole sport, or just the top teams and players? Do televised sports encourage people to get involved in sports, or do they have the opposite effect?

- Why do companies and advertisers use sports to sell their products? What is it about sports and star athletes that make them so popular with advertisers? Think about what sports stands for and what these athletes represent for the advertisers. Why do people buy things endorsed by an athlete?

- If you discovered a betting scandal had taken place in your sport, would it affect your view of the sport? How are sports undermined by betting and corruption? What should happen to athletes who are found to be involved in betting scandals?

- How do teams treat their fans? Do fans have a right to expect more loyalty from owners and players, or should they just accept that sports are a business? Do professional sports take loyal fans for granted?

- What would you most like to change about money and sports? How would you go about changing it? What impact would the change have?

GLOSSARY

advertiser person or business that uses advertising to promote their product or service

advertising way of drawing attention to a product or service by paying media such as television to include information designed to make the product look good

agent person who manages the business affairs and negotiates contracts for an athlete, in exchange for part of their earnings

amateur someone who is not paid for doing something, such as playing a sport

bookmaker person who takes bets on sporting events, calculates the chances of winning, and pays money back if the bet is successful

brand product made by a particular company, often with a distinctive mark to show who it is made by. Companies try to persuade people to think that their brands are better than other brands.

bribe money or gift that is given to persuade someone to do something or help the giver, often illegally

British Empire parts of the world ruled from Great Britain, particularly during the 1700s and 1800s

commerce business, or the buying and selling of goods and services

commercial relating to commerce and business

commissioner person who oversees U.S. sports such as baseball

corporate relating to corporations, companies, or businesses

corporation large company or business concern

cricket game played between two teams of 11 players that is popular in many places around the world, including Britain, Australia, New Zealand, South Asia, the Caribbean, and South Africa

developed country country where industry and the economy are fully developed. These are usually wealthier countries such as the United States, Britain, and Australia.

developing country country where the economy is not yet fully developed. Examples include many countries in Africa, Asia, and South America.

draft in U.S. sports, young players are recruited into professional teams from colleges in the yearly draft

elite best of something—such as athletes or teams—selected from a larger group

endorse give support to a product or person

endorsement paying someone, such as an athlete, to recommend, wear, or use a product

franchise business that has the right to promote itself as part of a larger group. In sports, a football team may promote itself as a franchise of the NFL.

Industrial Revolution major change and development in the industry of a country and development of factories. This happened first in Britain in the 1700s, followed by Europe, Japan, and the United States.

industry area of the economy concerned with a particular business

logo symbol designed to be a recognizable mark of a product or organization

marketing business of promoting or selling products and services

materialism valuing material possessions above spiritual values

media collective name for different means, or mediums of communication, such as newspapers, television, and the Internet

merchandise in entertainment and sports, items such as jerseys and other souvenirs that use the colors or image of a particular team or player

National Collegiate Athletic Association (NCAA) organization that oversees college sports in the United States, including organizing tournaments for sports such as basketball

Paralympics games for athletes with a disability, held after the Olympic Games in the same place

Premier League top professional soccer league in England

professional person who earns money for doing something, such as playing sports

replica something designed to be identical to the real thing, such as a replica sports shirt that matches the shirts worn by the team members themselves

rights ability or permission to do something. Companies buy television rights to give them permission to show a sporting event on television.

rugby rugby union is a game played by two teams of 15 players, popular in many countries around the world. Rugby league is a variation of the game for 13 players on each side.

salary regular payment that is made by an employer to an employee for the work the employee does

scholarship money given by a college to help pay for a student's education, often because the student excels academically or at sports

Soviet Union country that existed between 1922 and 1991, made up of Russia and 14 other republics, including Ukraine and Kazakhstan, which are all now separate countries

sponsor pay money to support something. Companies may sponsor an athlete or event as a form of advertising. The word is also used to describe the person or company doing the sponsoring.

strike protest in which workers refuse to work, usually because of a disagreement over pay or working conditions

NOTES ON SOURCES

THE ESSENCE OF SPORTS (pages 4–11)

1. The British Museum, "Sport in Ancient Greece: The Panathenaia Festival." http://www.britishmuseum.org/explore/families_and_children/online_tours/sport_in_ancient_greece/the_panathenaia_festival.aspx.
2. David Wallechinsky and Jaime Loucky, *The Complete Book of the Olympics* (London: Aurum Press, 2008), 10.
3. The British Museum, "Sport in Ancient Greece: Chariot Racing," http://www.britishmuseum.org/explore/families_and_children/online_tours/sport_in_ancient_greece/chariot_racing.aspx.
4. Keith Hopkins, "Murderous Games: Gladiatorial Contests in Ancient Rome," *History Today*, http://www.historytoday.com/keith-hopkins/murderous-games-gladiatorial-contests-ancient-rome.
5. Barbara F. McManus, "Arena: Gladiatorial Games," VRoma, http://www.vroma.org/~bmcmanus/arena.html.
6. *Encyclopædia Britannica*, s.v. "Sports," http://library.eb.co.uk/eb/article-253555.
7. *Encyclopædia Britannica*, s.v. "Sports," http://library.eb.co.uk/eb/article-253555.
8. Daniel Benjamin, "Traditions: Pro vs. Amateur," *Time*, July 27, 1992, http://www.time.com/time/magazine/article/0,9171,976117-1,00.html.
9. Wallechinsky and Loucky, *The Complete Book of the Olympics*, 31.
10. *Encyclopædia Britannica*, s.v. "Baseball," http://library.eb.co.uk/eb/article-30440.

WHO'S WHO IN MONEY AND SPORTS (pages 12–15)

1. "Real Madrid unfazed by row over Cristiano Ronaldo's image rights," *The Guardian*, June 17, 2009. http://www.guardian.co.uk/football/2009/jun/17/cristiano-ronaldo-real-madrid-image-rights-row.
2. BBC News, "Obituary: Mark McCormack," http://news.bbc.co.uk/sport1/hi/front_page/3035005.stm.

LIVING THE DREAM (pages 16–21)

1. The Tennis Times, "U.S. Open Will Become the World's Richest Tournament," http://thetennistimes.com/us-open-will-become-the-worlds-richest-tennis-tournament/.

2. Kurt Badenhausen, "The World's Highest-Paid Female Athletes," *Forbes*, August 18, 2010, http://www.forbes.com/2010/08/18/top-earning-female-athletes-business-sportsmoney-female-athletes.html.

3. "The World's 50 Top-Earning Athletes," *Forbes*, July 20, 2010, http://www.forbes.com/2010/07/20/most-valuable-athletes-and-teams-business-sports-sportsmoney-fifty-fifty-athletes_slide.html.

4. Badenhausen, "The World's Highest-Paid Female Athletes."

5. Eben Harrell, "Heroes: Didier Drogba," *Time*, April 29, 2010, http://www.time.com/time/specials/packages/article/0,28804,1984685_1984949_1985240,00.html.

6. "Wayne Rooney's New Contract 'contains targets for Manchester United'," *The Telegraph*, October 23, 2010, http://www.telegraph.co.uk/sport/football/players/wayne-rooney/8083397/Wayne-Rooneys-new-contract-contains-targets-for-Manchester-United.html.

7. WayneRooney.com, "Biography," http://www.wayne-rooney.org.uk/biography.html.

TEAM OR FRANCHISE? (pages 22–25)

1. *Encyclopædia Britannica*, s.v. "Football, gridiron," http://library.eb.co.uk/eb/article-234272.

2. *Wisden Cricketers' Almanac* (London: John Wisden and Co., 2008), 1372.

3. BBC News, "England Players Top IPL Auction," February 6, 2009, http://news.bbc.co.uk/sport1/hi/cricket/7871703.stm.

4. BBC News, "Glazer Wins Control of Man United," May 12, 2005, http://news.bbc.co.uk/1/hi/business/4540939.stm.

SPONSORS, ENDORSEMENTS, AND THE MEDIA (pages 26–33)

1. BBC News, "Tiger Woods Profile," November 27, 2009, http://news.bbc.co.uk/sport1/hi/golf/8383808.stm.

2. London 2012, "London 2012 Olympic Games Partners," http://www.london2012.com/about-us/the-people-delivering-the-games/international-and-uk-partners/index.php.

3. "Skateboarding Sponsorship FAQ," http://www.board-crazy.co.uk/skateboarding-sponsorship.php.

4. Nick Hoult, "How Allen Stanford's Twenty20 Cricket Dream Collapsed," *The Telegraph*, October 28, 2009, http://www.telegraph.co.uk/sport/cricket/6455333/How-Allen-Stanfords-Twenty20-cricket-dream-collapsed.html.

SPONSORS, ENDORSEMENTS, AND THE MEDIA (pages 26–33)

5. Ben Wyatt, "Could 2010 World Cup Final Be the Most Watched Event in History?" CNN, July 11, 2010, http://edition.cnn.com/2010/SPORTS/football/07/11/world.cup.final.television/index.htm.

6. Museum of Broadcast Communication, "Olympics and Television." http://www.museum.tv/eotvsection.php?entrycode=olympicsand.

FANS AND FOLLOWERS (pages 34–37)

1. Yahoosport, "NBA Average Ticket Prices Down 2 Years in a Row," November 24, 2010, http://uk.eurosport.yahoo.com/24112010/2/nba-average-ticket-prices-2-years-row.html.

2. Sean Leahy, "HD TV and Technology Pit NFL Stadiums vs. Fans' Living Rooms," *USA Today*, September 1, 2010, http://www.usatoday.com/sports/football/nfl/2010-08-31-nfl-hd-tv-stadium-or-living-room_N.htm.

3. "Dan Gilbert's open letter to fans: James' decision a 'cowardly betrayal' and owner promises a title before Heat," *Cleveland Plain Dealer*, July 8, 2010, http://www.cleveland.com/cavs/index.ssf/2010/07/gilberts_letter_to_fans_james.html.

4. Paul Kelso, "Wayne Rooney Blasts Angry England Fans," *The Telegraph*, June 18, 2010, http://www.telegraph.co.uk/sport/football/teams/england/7839649/Wayne-Rooney-blasts-angry-England-fans.html.

5. Daniel Howden, "Seats to Spare—But Fifa Won't Let South Africans Fill Them," *The Independent*, June 17, 2010, http://www.independent.co.uk/news/world/africa/seats-to-spare-ndash-but-fifa-wont-let-south-africans-fill-them-2002630.html.

THE STARS OF TOMORROW (pages 38–41)

1. *Encyclopædia Britannica*, s.v. "Basketball," http://library.eb.co.uk/eb/article-29671.

2. *Encyclopædia Britannica*, s.v. "Martina Hingis," http://library.eb.co.uk/eb/article-9488837.

3. BBC News, "Martina Hingis Statement in Full," November 1, 2007, http://news.bbc.co.uk/sport1/hi/tennis/7073908.stm.

4. Women's Tennis Association, 2011 Official Rulebook, 225–234.

5. Stuart James, "England's Young Footballers Face Final Whistle," *The Guardian*, June 12, 2010, http://www.guardian.co.uk/money/2010/jun/12/england-young-footballers-scrapheap.

SPORTS FOR EVERYONE (pages 42–45)

1. "Minor Leagues Hit the Mark," *New York Times*, July 28, 2002, http://query.nytimes.com/gst/fullpage.html?res=9B00E4DC173BF93BA15754C0A9649C8B63.
2. International Inspiration, http://www.london2012.com/get-involved/education/international-inspiration/index.php.

DIRTY MONEY (pages 46–49)

1. Alastair Jamieson, "Britain to Suffer Drop in Visitors During London 2012 Olympics," *The Telegraph*, September 12, 2010, http://www.telegraph.co.uk/sports/othersports/olympics/london2012/7996457/Britain-to-suffer-drop-in-visitors-during-London-2012-Olympics.html.
2. Jamieson, "Britain to Suffer Drop in Visitors."
3. Wallechinsky and Loucky, *The Complete Book of the Olympics*, 28.
4. "ICC bans Salman Butt, Mohammad Asif & Mohammad Amir," BBC News, February 5, 2011. http://news.bbc.co.uk/sport1/hi/cricket/other_international/pakistan/9388422.stm.
5. Sean Smith, "Corruption Probe: Bribe Scandals Threaten Punters on Beautiful Game," *The Financial Times*, December 9, 2010, http://www.ft.com/cms/s/0/4478486a-0261-11e0-ac33-00144feabdc0.html#axzz1AA3lBVmq.
6. Chicago History Museum, "History Files: Chicago Black Sox," http://www.chicagohs.org/history/blacksox.html.

THE FUTURE OF SPORTS AND MONEY (pages 50–53)

1. CBC News, "Bend It Like Beckham Airs on N. Korean TV," January 2, 2011, http://www.cbc.ca/arts/tv/story/2011/01/02/northkorea-beckham-film.html.
2. *Encyclopædia Britannica*, s.v. "Superbowl," http://library.eb.co.uk/eb/article-9070385.
3. Iain Carter, "Play-offs Pale in Shadow of Ryder Cup," BBC News, September 27, 2010, http://www.bbc.co.uk/blogs/iaincarter/2010/09/play-offs_pale_ion_shadow_of_r.html.

FIND OUT MORE

Books

Andrews, David. *Business Without Borders: Globalization (The Global Marketplace)*. Chicago: Heinemann Library, 2011.

Hensley, Laura. *Advertising Attack (Mastering Media)*. Chicago: Raintree, 2011.

Hunter, Nick. *Inside the Olympics*. Chicago: Heinemann Library, 2012.

Kerr, Jim. *Sports (Media Power)*. Mankato, Minn.: Amicus, 2011.

McLeish, Ewan. *Sports Industry (Closer Look: Global Industries)*. New York: Rosen, 2010.

Websites

Some of the best places to find out about money and sports are news websites. They report the latest stories on who earns what, in addition to giving the opinions of owners and fans. There are also sites that have in-depth coverage of particular sports.

Organizations representing individual sports have their own websites, such as the following:

www.nfl.com
This is the website of the National Football League (NFL).

www.nba.com
This is the website of the National Basketball Association (NBA).

www.mlb.com
This is the website of Major League Baseball.

www.olympic.org
This website includes lots of detail about the Olympic Games and also gives links for more information about Olympic sports.

Individual teams and athletes may also have their own websites. To be sure that you are finding reliable information, check that the site is official.

Places to visit

Many sports teams and organizations have museums that tell the history of the team or sports. Some also offer the chance to visit their stadium to find out how the business of sports works off the field.

If you have a chance to attend a sporting event, whether it is the Olympics or just your local team playing, you can find out about how money is involved in the event.

- How many people are watching? Have they all paid for tickets? Look to see if there are television cameras or reporters at the event.

- Is there any merchandise for sale? It might be someone selling programs and snacks, or there could be a huge store selling all kinds of branded goods.

- Is there any advertising in the stadium or on the players' clothing?

All these things can tell you more about the role of money in your favorite sports.

Suggestions for further research

There are many other topics in sports and business that you can explore to develop your knowledge of money and sports. Here are a few suggestions:

- This book has considered the effects of money on a variety of sports, particularly the most high-profile team sports. You could investigate how money affects your favorite sports. It could be one of the professional sports covered in this book, or an amateur sport where there are no highly paid players and endorsements.

- Learn more about the history of the Olympic Games. From small beginnings, the Olympics have become the world's most successful and expensive sporting event. Find out about the history of the Games, including the battle to keep the Games amateur and the impact of professionals on the Olympics.

- Discover more about how the media presents sports, from the technology to the words and techniques that are used to make sports appealing and exciting. You can also find out about whether the media focus on a narrow range of sports that excludes women's sports and less popular sports.

- Endorsements and advertising are a major source of money that goes into sports. Find out more about the techniques that advertisers use to sell their products. The more you know, the easier it is to spot when those techniques are being aimed at you.

INDEX